UNTAMED WHISPERS

Emotions penned down in verses...from my heart to you.

VINITA BICHOLKAR

Copyright © <Published Year><Author Name>

Made with ❤ on the Notion Press Platform

www.notionpress.com

To those who shaped me. This book is dedicated to my loved ones who have touched my heart, mind and soul. Your presence in my life has inspired the words within these pages . To the whispers within that made me write the words in this book. May they resonate with those who reads them.

Contents

Foreword

Poetry, for me, is more than just words—it's the way I observe, imagine, and translate emotions onto a page. Some feelings are lived, some are only sensed, but through my words, they all feel as if they've been experienced.

Whether it's love, longing, or life itself, I let my poetry speak, not of what I've been through, but of what I can make you feel.

Preface

As I sit down to reflect on the journey of creating this collection of poems, it showed me the power of observations and the beauty of the human experiences. The words that flow through these pages are a testament to the whispers of my heart, shaped by my observations, emotions and experiences.

I have always been drawn to the world of words where feelings and thoughts are blend together with imaginary tales in a delicate dance. And so, this collection, 'Untamed Whispers', is a reflection of my inner world, where the boundaries of reality and imagination blur.

The poems within these pages explore themes that are close to my heart; self-love, self-worth, and the intricacies of social and societal issues, They delve into complexities of love and romance, and the quiet moments of beauty and nature that punctuate our daily lives.

Hoping these poems to resonate to those who love reading and those love deeply-especially young adults and adults who find meaning in love, self- dicovery and the world around them as much as I do.

Acknowledgments

Writing this book has been one of the most rewarding and challenging experiences of my life, and I couldn't have done it alone.

To my parents, thank you for everything.

To the people who reminded me that stories deserve to be told, even the quiet ones—thank you for your silent encouragement.

To Notion Press Publishing for being the platform that made this book possible.

And to ChatGPT, for assisting me in editing my book smoothly.

Prologue/Introduction

This book consists of themes like Love Tales, inward bloom, breaking the barriers, musings and whispers and terra verde

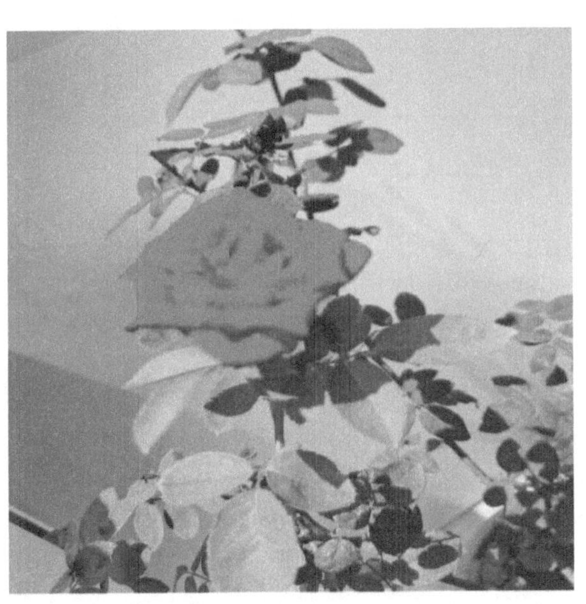

1. LOVE TALES

WARM LOVE LIKE FIRE
Pure love is like fire, keeping you and your soul warm
after ages.
It protects you from the cold outside.
Every day, it's a bonfire night for you to enjoy the
winters.

It burns the unwanted clutter you once carried.
It cleanses you from within.
A fire that pushes you to burn and do something—
Your body feels renewed.

AFTER A LONG TIME
Oh! How do I tell you that when I saw you,
I forgot whether the moon had come or the sun?

I saw the rain coming washing away everything I faced.
Your eyes held a solitaire diamond ring that shined
when you saw people and smiled.

These miles don't count when it's you—
because you are bigger than distance for us and our love.

Waiting for you is the sweetest ache I've ever known.
While watching you, I screamed, and tears came out
with a screeched voice.
My hormones get extra love when I see you...
The love that heals the imbalances they hold.

RED HUES OF LOVE
Oh! To love you is like wearing my favorite red dress
time and again,
like placing red roses in my hair every day!

It's like a red velvet cake I relish for a lifetime,
like drinking Roohafza daily without waiting for summer
to arrive.

It's like storing strawberries for the whole season
so I can eat them happily.

It's like tying a red ribbon in my hair,
so I can look like the prettiest girl with curls too.

It's like eating fresh watermelon in the summer loo.
It's like watching the breathtaking red sunset whenever
it arrives.

It's like stopping at a red traffic light,
so I can be safe.

It's like double tapping a red heart on the most heart-
touching messages on WhatsApp.
Oh, to love you is to forever wear my heart in red.

HUES SMEARED

I had basic colors in my life—
greens, orange sunset hues,
white with my bunny teeth grin.

But the colors that would smear my cheeks,
making me blush hard, were not there...
Until you arrived.

You smeared my cheeks red,
making sure I smeared it back at you.

You showed me that love was more than the red I saw in
the movies.
It was soft pastel pink when you were gentle with me.
It was white when I needed silence.
It was yellow when you smiled brighter than Mr. Sun
outdoors.

It was purple when your soul smelled like mild lavender
perfume.
You showed me I could love black too—
embracing my dark shadows,
yet you would still love me anyway.

I got all my hues on my cheeks,
and in my life, smeared by you and your love...

Now, I don't bother about my white clothes getting stained,
because I'll be loved by you deeply and still look pretty!

GOLD MINE HEART

Oh! How to tell you that your heart is Amazon's forest gold —
The way you make space for others has my whole heart.
The way you wear your heart on your sleeves—
I want to kneel down with my heart in hand, for you, in front of you.
The way your heart beats for everything around.
The machine would also not calculate it properly.
Because doctors would claim you a rare piece too!
So think about me—the way I can't believe that you exist...
Your heart is literally big—if opened, the rose will fall off fresh.
The way kindness is literally you as the face of it.
The way honesty exists because you breathe...
The sunflower field lost one sunflower—
Because that just got transported among us—between you and me, and among humans.

SUNDOWN WEDDINGS

Sundown weddings are the prettiest ones.
Because you can literally skip the makeup
And glow naturally in the sun's golden hour...

The glow of getting married to the love of your life
Is seen on your face.
Making the sun bow down in love with the couple
And turning the sundown into a showstopper!

The bride walks down the aisle
With the happiest tears in her eyes,
Seeing that the sun will shine even brighter,
Giving her all the deserved spotlight of her entire
lifetime.

She might have planned everything right .
But her fairytale wedding dream comes true
When the sun shows its gorgeous hues.

Her lehenga gets the natural limelight,
Leaving us bowled over for a long time.
Guests get lost in their aesthetic picture game.
Then , shower the couple with a rain of rose petals.

To see the groom happily crying and embracing her
tight,
The sun will almost blush and hide behind the green
bush,
Waiting until everything settles into the party mood—
For the after effects of every wedding
That happens in the sundown glow.

ANSWERED PRAYERS
I prayed for happiness to hold my fingers—
You came in...

When I asked for comfort after years,
You settled in my soul, keeping me warm.

I asked for roses to make me blush with their hues—
You came in, being the rose
That now I write poetry about!

I asked for peace once—
You became the peace that my pieces were craving...

I asked, What in the world can I call mine, finally?
He replied, I'm yours in ways that can't be defined...

Will I ever experience excitement that makes me cry
happily?
He smiled back, saying,
Haven't you felt it every time you look at me, darling?

Will I ever be able to tell the things that make me the
happiest—
Without being cut off?
Now, I write letters to him,
And he reads…

NEVER STOPPING TO LOVE YOU
I'll never stop loving you—
Because if I did, I'd lose myself again...

Not because I'm dependent,
But because I learn to live fully by loving you.

Where my breath is not faster,
My chest is not tight anymore ...
Where my laughter is constant—
Because it's you.

My home is you now—
So if I don't love you the way I do,
I'll lose my soul's only roof...

My shield is the strength
That comes from loving you.
I tried to fit in,
But with you, I belong to my safest place.

Loving you untangles the thread of things
That holds me back...

I'll never stop loving you—
Because it's my only peace.
The only excitement
That leaves me breathless sometimes...

While I thrive and heal when I love you,
It's my source of existing the way I crave to.
I'll never stop loving you—
Because that's where I'm sanely alive!

MY ONLY ONE
Oh! To love you like my only moon crescent,
my only favorite present…
The reason why I randomly scream with tears in my
eyes.

Oh! I get to love you when you exist beyond all the
phases of getting to see you!
Because loving you is like reading my favorite poetry on
loop—for all the right feelings.

LOVE LIKE A ROSE SHADOW

The shadow of your love—
protecting me like a rose's shadow.

Making sure I can see myself—
the way I have always longed to.
Making sure I look up boldly—
because I'm just learning to live by…

Because if he doesn't make me believe
that just one person is enough to lean on—
I'll dry off, like scattered rose petals on the ground.

He's watering my growth,
My roots are getting loved by you finally.

You can't separate a shadow.
Neither does it leave you—
even if you want it to.
That's him to me!

The rose can face herself—
because her shadow is too pretty to ignore.
That's him to me!

The shadow of the rose watches her bloom,
leaning too close,
and smiles with a smirk.
That's him to me!

STORM THAT CHANGED EVERYTHING
You don't get it—
how impossible it is to see yourself,
after years of seeing yourself through others' lenses—
until a storm arrives—
clearing the polluted air,
so you can finally breathe.

Like a wind beneath my wings,
you arrived—
pushed me to soar high.

No intentions.
Just pure support.

That day was the beginning—
of everything I ever dreamt of.

Stars and starlight,
under the same moon.
Games of words played together—
as poets too.

SOULMATE

Your soulmate is your best friend,
With whom you can crash down, and he will hold you.
Where you can just sit next to him, doing your thing,
And yet, feel you are home.

We can talk a lot, but with him, you can shhh! yourself.
Calm rises like a dove in your organs.
Comfort is given without asking.
Emptiness dries out,
And you feel all the colors in your life again.

Your eyes shine because you are truly loved!
You can hear him whisper affirmations
That your existence truly needs.
Breathing becomes softer, more relaxed.
More than lovers, beyond partners—
Your soul is tied to an invisible thread,
Knowing, without uttering a word.

LIP BALM × LOVE

Lip balm soothes our lips and their skin.
Likewise, love does the same to our soul, enriching it.

Lip balm heals our cracked lips.
Love heals our cracked heart,
Working deep to nourish it.

Patience lets lip balm work its magic.
Likewise, love needs time, effort, and patience.
Both are curated, considering what's needed—
Soft enough to heal,
Helping you grow,
Or liberate you.

Both have healing properties.

STARDUST

You met me when I was fading,
Almost into the dust of the crowd.

I became stardust when you came in,
Lighting up everything that was shut for so long.
Didn't know how to process it back then…

Now, I know how to hold it,
Never letting you go.
Leaving everything else
That ceases me from loving you.

LITTLE BIT MORE
I fall in love with you a little bit more,
Like water slowly poured into a glass.

Like waves brushing your ankles,
Unaware.

Like sunrises and all the sunsets on my balcony.
Like my favorite song playing on loop.
Like rose petals falling into my lap.
Like clear skies and rains throughout the years.

Every second,
Every day,
Every 365 days of my years—
I fall in love with you a little bit more.

MY BELOVED ROSE
I always wanted roses around,
But I never knew you would become the roses to my
hair.

Your love made me glow as I grew.
Nothing bothers me now—
Because I have you for life.

The way you hold my hair .
 because you are my only rose , you hold my soul too.
Sometimes, you are the roses in my hair,
And sometimes, the fragrance that lingers in my soul.

You revolve in my mind,
The way the scent of roses never fades.
I guess I'm falling for you—
The way I fall for red roses every day.

YOU KISSED MY SCARS…

I loved myself, and you loved me with the scars that I
have.
I was tripping and falling every day, but you made me
fall for you every day.

I doubted myself.
My hollow darkroom was the only thing I had—
Dark and all pretended, when all I wanted was to show
who I was for real.

You untied the knot of my soul that was not needed,
And you tied the knot with my soul that was much
needed.

I wondered whether I was loved, but you showed me
what I deserved in love!

My existence was full of things done for me as a favour
.
But you added love to my life as my only flavor.

FEELING THAT KEEPS YOU ALIVE

Some feelings are so strong that they tear you apart to
bring you back, making you feel alive.
That makes you cry in happiness, which heals you.

The feeling that brings out the best in you—sometimes,
you cannot handle that feeling, which makes you happily
overwhelmed.

Where people think you are going crazy,
when this is the only feeling that makes you insanely
sane.
Your wounds heal , you smile and cry at the same time.

With this feeling in your heart, you want to cry out and
say, "Yaasss!! This is healing me!"

You can't express and explain it,
but it's called love—from a pure soul—
that makes the other person also feel truly loved ,
keeping you alive.

THINKING ABOUT YOU

I can't stop thinking about you because you are an
imprint on my soul.
Thinking about you on a loop makes my overthinking
melt like butter on a pan.

I can't stop thinking about you because I want to replay
everything I know about you,
gaining a PhD and doing research on you...

Oh! Because you are my only reason to keep my mind
charged!
I can't stop thinking about you because every detail
about you is my treasure to hold for long.

WHITE BOUGAINVILLEA AND YOU

A gentle breeze...
Like a bunch of white Bougainvillea growing at the side
of the street,
Still, they stood out for me.

In the same way,
 you walked into my life.
  Swayed me off my feet,
standing out even if you have the same flesh and blood
as others.

White Bougainvillea adds color to any scene around—
Likewise, you did the same for me.
White Bougainvillea has been adding to my smiles often,
just like you have been doing since the time you met me!

COME TO THE GARDEN MY LOVE
Come to the garden, my love.
I want to see the moon with you every single night,
showing my face to you too—
how it lights up when I see you after a long time.

If you want, I'll wear your favorite aftershave,
the one that lingers in your soul a little longer.
I can't wait to see you in that kurta,
the one I first saw you in,
with those tiny pearl earrings,
 that make you look even softer—
as if you were made for me only.

Let's talk about how we met,
and stayed a little longer than we thought.
Let's show the moon that we can dance under its light,
carefree and swift!

Slowly, she whispered,
"Can we come after years of our togetherness too?"

He smiled and said,
"Yes... This place gave me thousands of reasons
to look at you the way I do,
and I wouldn't want any other place
for the moon to witness this—
and everything that we are, my darling."

IF NOT YOU, THEN WHO?
The intimacy of "if not you, then no one"
is such a blessing to the one loved like that!

In a world full of options and convenience,
you are the only one I want to love.

No, it's not settling for less;
it's finding home in someone who brings you peace.

It's something you gave that I won't leave
for things that don't make sense to me after this...

You love chocolate cake,
so why would you choose pineapple cake one day?

It's your being that matches my soul,
not some exchange offer you get in the market!

"If not you, then no one else"—
the kind of love people crave to get.

Oh, to love you is already fulfilling;
why would I settle the way you think I will?

BURNING IN YOUR AURA
I gulped down the burn I felt,
watching you wrapped in that midnight elegance.
Something ran through my veins,
tears welled up in my eyes—
a feeling of something coming to life,
beyond dreams, into reality.

The way your aura shined
with nothing but a walk,
I held my breath at every glimpse that I saw .

What even in the world—that you are so damn
breathtaking?
I lost all the words,
and my tears spoke volumes.
I stare, just to breathe enough
for another attack.

People talk about attention,
but I give you my whole existence
just to watch you breathe.

Every time I think I've reached
the peak of my scream,
the next one comes louder—
with tears that, if stopped,
would steal the air from my lungs.

A dangerous sight,
yet a breathtaking beauty.

COLOURED IN YOUR LOVE, RETURNED TO MYSELF

The way I'm already a gone case,
the way I forget hours when I'm with you—
because you don't count the peaceful hours spent...

The way silence speaks volumes between us,
You are the season of my love.
Someone stole my heart,
and love took over with its hues!

Eyes spoke everything we didn't.
Since the time I met you,
my paths have cleared—
for me to walk, jump, and run—oh my God!

What I was before you,
I can't remember it now.
But who I am today
was once just a dream.

Coloured in your love,
yet returned to myself—finally, for sure.
Colour me in orange sunset hues,
the way your love holds me still.

TABLE FOR TWO
This time, it was different.
She led him to his seat, hand in hand, soft and familiar.
Their eyes met, a silent conversation between souls as they
walked together.

They sat, each gaze lingering, asking the unspoken question,
"Shall we?"
She nodded, her heart knowing,
and gently took his hands, caressing them,
releasing the weight of past years
while living fully in the beauty of this moment.

A table set with pancakes, pizzas,
but the food was almost forgotten,
as their eyes stayed locked,
mouths full yet hearts open,
speaking in the silence between bites.

Was it their first date?
No, it was their anniversary,
but the way they gazed,
it could have been their first.
Three decades, and still, their love glowed with the same
warmth,
as if no time had passed at all.

A table for two,
candles flickering,
the soft rhythm of the waves in the distance,
bare feet dancing on a sandy beach,
no words needed, just the sway of love in the air.

Their love had waited,
endured, and bloomed.
In every gaze, they found each other again, and again.

LIGHT OF MY LIFE
The darkness I knew existed,
You became the light that I never knew I needed.
Like a scented candle, you filled my life with fragrance,
Turning me once again into someone romantic.

This candle of mine beats with a heart full of kindness
and grace,
Guiding those who need light in their lives.
Just as you knew the light and guidance I needed,
Your presence illuminated my path ahead.

The hope you gave me with your light
Will forever fuel my fight.

FLIGHT TO HOME
When you finally breathe like you haven't before,
It feels like catching a flight—
as if, if not caught, you will miss it.

It happens when you are finally seen.
But with time, you will learn
that calm breaths will come often now—
because after years, darling,
you are finally home,
to your forever right sight.

I BELONG TO YOU

I belong to you, like snow belongs to the mountains.
I belong to you, like candles belong to the flames of
fire.
I belong to you, like cookies belong with tea in the
evening.
I belong to you, like summer belongs to a summer cooler
drink.
I belong to you, like a coffee bean belongs to one pot of
coffee.
I belong to you, like a fairytale belongs to my reality.
I belong to you, like an ocean belongs to its end.
I belong to you, like we belong to each other.

COLOUR ME IN YOUR LOVE

Colour me in your love—
because that's how I'll learn about colours and their hues.

I saw colours but never felt it…
until you arrived!

Now, I see rainbows too—
and capture them, smiling wide at them.

Roses now smell divine—
because I have one now...
watering it every day, so that I breathe fresh.

My anklets dance—
to the way my heart beats for you.

MOONLIT LONGING
You can feel the moon, but you can't touch it when you
crave.
The distance feels unbearable—
but it's harder when a moon lover
can't see the moon every night.

Sink it in or capture it,
before there's a gap between you and the moon again…
Oh! How to explain the ache
that runs from your chest to your ribs, deep inside…

No matter what you do,
until you see the moon,
until you feel it the way you want,
you won't sip your juice and relax!

Logic and feelings don't align—
just like your heart and mind.

WHEN LOVE ARRIVES
The one who ever felt like home was always somewhere
in the world.
Someone who stepped into her life,
when she was tearing apart, tripping hard—
 Love caught her in time, her breath held delicately.

She never felt the wind before,
but he made her feel that too…
because he came in,
with her favorite music—
the sound of being loved the way she deserved.

Oh! To be loved by someone
who understands the world
in the most accepting way!

She wasn't ready for good things yet,
but he became too good to be true—just for her!

Now, tell her—if this isn't meant to be, then what is?
When peace has finally become a person for her,
do you really think her heart
could long for anything else beyond this?

THE MIRROR KNOWS
The mirror saw the way she loved him.
She cried happily when she saw him for a little longer,
just trying to believe that she got someone so precious.

How she screamed with overwhelming tears of having
him...
How she danced, looking in the mirror, for having him...
How she was quirky all the time,
how she acted carefree,
how she always got lost in her thoughts that made her
smile...

When she caught herself smiling,
she laughed hard then.
How she screamed as if she was going to die without
breathing—
the scream that made her alive again!

Oh! The way her cheeks flushed while talking about
him,
looking in the mirror...
She cried in shock of having him,
pulling her blushed cheeks—
and it was all gone.

The mirror had never seen her like this before.
So, it always listened, witnessed her happy glow,
blessed her,
and stood where she always returned
to say more—every day, often.

SMASHING THROUGH
Smashing—when he stands tall,
fixing his sleeves, adjusting his collar,
grinning at people with that effortless charm.
Ahh! Her heart flips a thousand miles away!

Absolutely smashing—
with that soft smile on his face,
genuine enough to melt her molten lava inside,
without eruption!

Smashing—when he moves with ease,
soft and smooth like a marshmallow,
melting people into the puddle of his existence.

He smashed her—
with those deep brown eyes,
holding steady, knowing too much,
looking in as if they had always known.

Do one thing—
smash everything at once and smirk,
because he won.
Undeniably, a smasher!

LOVE THAT LETS YOU BE
The way you love me—nobody can.
The way you comfort me through your deep eyes,
as if I've reached my calm shores.

My rope of hope that you are,
gives me immense strength to go ahead
and live freely...

Silences are never awkward between us.
The way you saw me,
I saw myself after that—truly.

Reassurances are common here, like fireflies.
Through you, I realized
that love is not always loud...
And that's the most comforting truth
I have ever encountered.

Love like that just lets you be,
while they silently stitch roses with their love
onto the deep-cut wounds
you once carried.

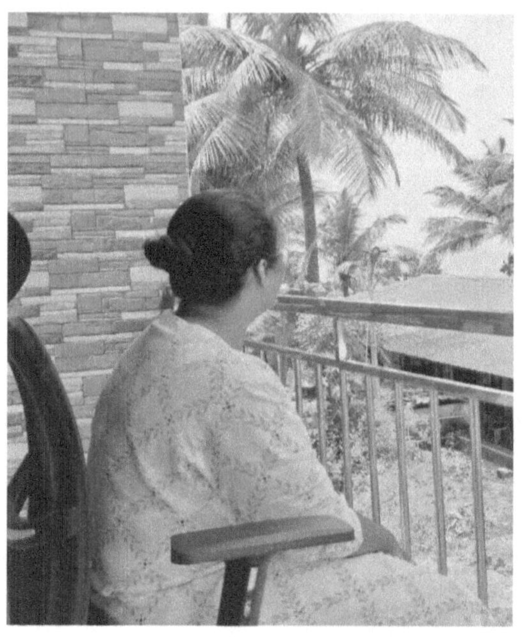

2. INWARD BLOOM

For you to bloom, you will have to choose where and how you want to bloom.

\-   *VINI*

FIRE WITHIN ME
Like fire, I burn inside with everything that holds me back.
Fire in my eyes keeps me sane.

Oh! How do I tell you?
Every day, I walk on flames to barely survive!
The burns everywhere remind me of how people have failed me.

My soul tells me I am made of fire entirely!
But lately, I am melting before the snow melts.
If the fire within me is extinguished,
I will surely perish.

HAPPINESS THAT BLOOMS MY SOUL

I dreamt of a garden of twelve dancing princesses...
Because those who have it are said to be living their best
lives.

Until I realized that you can have one too,
If you include all the things that make you twirl in
happiness.

Your greens, sunset viewing, taking selfies,
And dancing—even in your normal shoes!
Releasing your stress in greens, roaming on your terms...
All these lead you toward your magic garden of peace
and happiness.
Now, I tend to my own magic garden, where happiness
blooms forever.

8TH MARCH MAGIC

The way the wind kissed my hair that evening

When I went to celebrate myself that day.
The way my skin felt the love of my beloved greens.
The way the sunset spread its hues when I came,
As if bowing down in my glory.

Bougainvillea in my chariot,
Adorning me with grace.
The moon on top glanced at me and blushed...
They assembled to see the queen that arrived,
Who loved them too much for their existence.

The way she breathes with them,
And does not treat them as her only background score...
is just wow !

STRETCH MARKS: A SIGN OF BRAVERY
Stretch marks are the body's way of reacting
To the major physical changes a woman goes through—
Be it pregnancy or weight gain.

They deepen when you eat something that can increase them later…
Some get them all over their body,
Always itchy, uncomfortable.

They don't go away if they're too much.
Some live with them,
Some become extremely conscious—
Stop wearing sleeveless tops,
Not showing skin at all.

Not everyone accepts them,
Because they're not part of the "ideal" body.
But they weren't there by birth, so why the shame?
And when they become permanent, let's slay!

Your skin is for you to form, not for others to see.
I agree, there are days when you touch and see—
But see them with pride, please!

Because only two people will see you with them...
It's you first !
And the other one will see your soul first, then your body—
So please, don't worry!

Focus on the first person—
That's you, in the mirror, accepting yourself.
The second one will come only if you agree.
Otherwise, please don't worry! Stretch marks are here to show you your bravery,
Not to stop you from living, but to remind you of your strength.

FLOWER IN HER HAIR
A flower in her hair is her way to slay the day.
The scent of her hair flirts with the flower,
Adorned in her hair so boldly!

She will scream for her victory...
Her hair becomes the stage for the flower,
Performing its duty—making her look like a sundar
stree.

The flower tells her nature's story,
And her hair tells the years of her age-old misery.
But the way both heal each other
Is beyond beautiful, beyond imagination...

The scars and the scent of the flower,
Tucked in her hair—
A hat trick of beauty!

HORMONAL DOUBLE SHIFTS

There are days when your hormones want to dance—as
if you won lakhs in your wallet!
Sweating and dancing till you wonder— what's wrong
with me?

And then there are days when your hormones want you
to fire someone—
without even knowing why!

It happens monthly for all women,
but it happens regularly to those with PCOS.
Some days, you will shower rose petals on people;
other days, you will splash water directly in their faces…

But through it all—
you have to just look after yourself.
Yes, only you!

Because you saw others for too long,
somewhere losing yourself along the way,
leading to this.

Now?
Treat yourself like you exist in your own empire.
Cater to your needs like a queen in power!

You want to twirl?
Go ahead—twirl in your favorite dress.
Want to sulk?
Do it—till you get bored of it.

The point is—
don't mask yourself just to fit in.
Find and stick to those who get you—
even when you're lashing out at your moods.

POETRY IN PLEATS
Poetry in pleats, it is.

Look how it drapes around your body—
hugging your curves,
whispering—
"Hey! You are loved.
You look pretty!"

Comforting you with its fabric,
making you look elegant—
just by being on you.

A simple piece of cloth—
turned breathtaking—
because you wear it.

No matter who you are—
you make pleats look poetry in motion, darling.

No restrictions—
on how you wear it.
What size?
It doesn't matter.

With gajra or without.
Kajal in your eyes, or not.
Bindi on your forehead, or not.
Earrings, or not.

It still looks fabulous—
because you wear it,
Sundar Mahila.

TWIRL ON WHEELS
Twirling on wheels might not make sense,
Because on feet, it's all glorified.
But what if you don't get to decide?
What do you do then?

Cry in corners,
Or swirl yourself the way you can?

You can't decide everything,
But you can decide how you do it.
Work should be done,
Whether feeling like twirling or being a princess—
You do it with grace.
And that's when it's unique and magnificently seen.

GIRLS ARE BORN TO SLAY!
A girl child is not just a gender to say,
Rather, a chance for your generations to slay!

Let it not be a day's celebration,
It should be the foundation of progressive years ahead.

The moment you carry a girl child in your arms,
Remember, a warrior—when needed—has arrived.
But before that, a human is born.

Let her bloom,
You just need to water her growth.
She will do wonders,
If loved unconditionally.

FLOWERS AND THE QUEEN
She adorned the flowers of her dreams,
But she was a flower herself—
A bloom of grace and kindness.

She saw the world with utmost softness,
Which was mistaken for weakness.
But she knew what softness meant,
Because she never received it.

Oh! The flowers in her hair were lucky to be her
happiness,
They made her happy—without conditions.
That's why she loved them unconditionally.

Oh! To be loved by her
Was nothing short of feeling like a queen.
But she was the real queen.

CROWN YOURSELF UP!
Crown yourself up when nobody calls you a queen.
Crown yourself up when you achieve something—small
or big.
Crown yourself up when you find solutions to your
worries.
Crown yourself up when you feel like giving up, yet you
get up.
Crown yourself up when you grow,
Even while being criticized and mocked.

THAT'S ENOUGH!

Plus size or normal size, it doesn't matter.
As long as you have a normal beating heart with plus love inside.

Fair or not so fair, be grateful that life is being fair to you!
Stretch marks or no stretch marks, if you can stretch yourself enough to keep your body healthy, that's enough!

Pimples or dry skin—if your skin is disease free, that's enough!
If you have a healthy mind, emotions, and body, that's enough!

Whenever people comment on your body ,
 say, "That's enough now!"
And walk away, respecting yourself with love—enough to survive!

You were enough for your creator, and that should be enough for you too!

SAY HELLO, BEAUTIFUL!
Look in the mirror and say hi to yourself every day.
Say, "Hello, beautiful! You are really doing great!"

Listen to your heart, less to your brain.
Say hello to your soul, because that's one of a kind—
healing from the bruises, still alive.

People will have opinions, because they have inner
beauty blindness.
You stay focused because you know your worth,
because you are your own guide.

GIRL WITH A BUN
The girl with a bun doesn't do it for the hairstyle.
She just wants to shed her past of not being herself.

She wants to be guilt free for not choosing herself in the
past .
When she ties her hair up, she's assuring herself that now
it's her time to step ahead.

It's her time to build her life the way she wants to.
She doesn't want to burden her shoulders with more
guilt, insecurities, and overthinking.
She found herself again—herself, truly.
It's the freedom that every girl wants.

Now, when she leaves her hair, it's not under any
pressure anymore...
just her way to let her curls feel the freedom she got.

She leaves her hair this time because she will never let
her freedom go into the wrong hands anymore.
She's confident this time—truly herself.

UNBEARABLE HAPPINESS
Under the sun, she got tanned after ages, which was
beyond the glow without it.
How the sunset made her believe that it belongs to the
greens,
made her think how her favorite things belonged to the
glow because of the same.

If she needed that peace of being truly seen,
she should stay close to the things that gave her
happiness—unexplained.
The happiness that failed her words to come to her
tongue
but never failed to come in her poems effortlessly!

If unbearable struggles were in her fate,
let her also have unbearable happiness to balance it too.

MORE THAN YOU THINK
You are so much more than you think—
more than what you do, more than what you can,
more than just handling expectations.

Everything that you are is not tied to the service you
provide;
it's a byproduct of what you put in, not who you are.

You are the person who smiles when someone
compliments you,
the way you carry yourself in a crowd.
You are human first, and then anything the world would
prefer you to be.

YOU ARE VALID!
Even if you don't understand someone,
don't disrespect them!
Even if you think differently,
don't pull others down!
Knowingly or unknowingly, when people hurt you
constantly,
don't say they didn't know what they were up to!
If at all you realize that you are being wronged
somehow,
focus on healing and growing.
Remember and remind yourself—
you are doing it for yourself,
because others did it for themselves
when you were hurting yourself step by step!
You heal,
when you know few people who truly see you will
always be there for you,
but be there for yourself too!
It's the only balance you need.

GIRL WITH A RIBBON IN HER HAIR
Ribbon tied in her hair shows her strength to face the
world.
The sparkle in her eyes lights up the stars in the sky!
Knowing that it won't be easy for her,
 until she becomes tough yet soft with her kindness.

Seeking a chance from the world yet grabbing her
opportunities to stand in the same world!
Her smile is her weapon, at times taken for granted as
her weakness.

Why can't her soul be soft yet burning with fire to
achieve something?
Why should her personality fit into a regular mold,
When she deserves what she wants and gets it by her
hard work!

You praise her or not, she's still worth beyond every
norm, no matter the praise or silence!

WHEN NOISE AROUND YOU TAKES OVER!
It's not that she doesn't know
about the crown she deserves—
She knows the things she did.

But the voices around her
were so loud for years...

That one seed of doubt, planted deep,
played its role without warmth around.
She believed she needed more.

Voices from the outside were loud,
even when everything inside her
was full of love.
You start believing them,
and suddenly, you feel
you are not enough...

But what if everything around you,
inside and out,
was filled with bullets continuously?
Would you still believe in yourself then?

The voices need to be reduced
so you can hear yourself,
gain support,
and walk ahead.

All theories and tips don't work

until you see an environment
where you can grow.

If you can look in the mirror
and see yourself as beautiful,
something within you will shift.

So, you need people
who can be your mirror—
helping you see yourself fully.

FROM SURVIVAL TO DESTINY
When you really want something,
there will be extreme obstacles—
as if making you doubt whether you truly deserve it.

Making you wonder, when did it become so difficult?
Is it because what you want is so precious
that people are ready to tear it apart?

But if you know you don't want to leave this earth
before it happens…
Then something is definitely brewing in heaven to make
it happen.

If, in all the dysfunction ,
this is the only thing helping you to function,
then why wouldn't it happen
to let you move forward beyond survival?

Dysfunction around you can tease
the only thing that keeps you going,
but can they really stop
what needs to happen for you to be functional at least?

CHANGE WITHIN

We can be vocal about change,
But we, as women,
Need to change the way we look after ourselves.

You want to breathe?
Go to the park and do it.
You need to dance?
Join a dance class, please.

If you need to ask to breathe,
Change the place—
Not your breathing style, please...

Nobody asks men about their choices.
If you are asked,
Don't reply—just walk off toward your dreams!

Water can be still for a while,
But there will be movement in it!
When you feel the time is up,
And you are done with it already...
Go ahead and choose a different path!

If you can't move,
Create your own space within—
Work on your skills and mental peace.
There will be a way out
If you have the will towards your forever bliss.

MAGIC IN HER EYES
She laughed because she knew what would happen next.
Oh! She smirked after knowing the effect...

Her eyes had the magic of finding magic ,
in everything she encountered.

She appeared soft because she valued it,
but her soul smelled of iron when heated.

When needed, she turned fire into a bonfire—
fireflies in the dark.

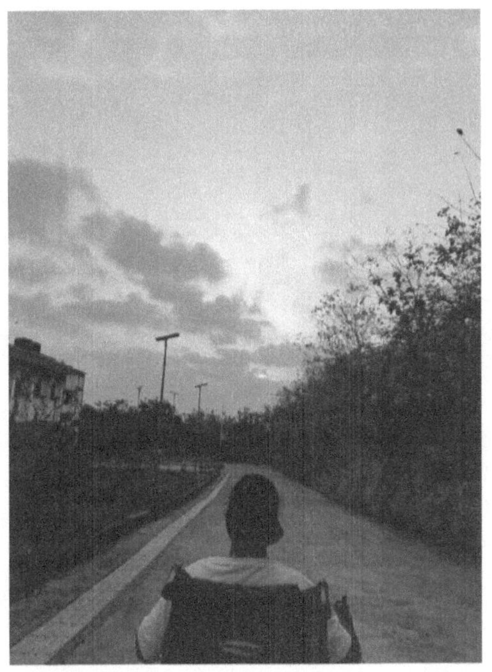

3. BREAKING THE BARRIERS

WHEELS CONTRASTS
On wheels, she tries to live her best.
But years later, she's on an important quest—
How long will she be on it?
Just to say, I'm different and embracing it with grace...

Should she forget how these very wheels can't surpass
every mountain bliss—
And the staircase place?
Ramps are not everywhere, so she drops her dreamy
favorite place...
What's within reach for you—is far for her.
By the time she reaches there, it might be too late.

But she deserved better.
In tried and tested fact—
She lost some basics which you can't even think of
losing...

Sitting and getting pushed on wheels is not a luxury
darling.
It's my way of saying, bring it on—because you can't
break what's already broken.

I try to see my soul so that I don't see the wheels...
Wheels are my surviving tool—not my superpower all
the time exactly!

WHAT DO YOU MEAN BY CHOOSING YOUR HAPPINESS?

How do you decide how many times
You get to choose your happiness?
Because each time you choose it,
It will be your first—according to you.

Is there an end line to really choosing yourself?
Or is it just being selfish all the time?
Society thinks she is selfish because she did this,
But tell me—
What is the criteria for choosing yourself and your
happiness?

There is no end to it, darling...
It's a loop—once in, never out.
Everything right is wrong somewhere.
Everything right is wrong in most places.
So no real end—
And it's your end, then truly.

The simple way out—
If you truly, truly feel the happiest
Around what you chose, then that's it!
No more ifs and buts.

Because that one choice
Can keep someone alive and living...
You don't know what freedom means to each.
You chose your freedom,
And then you came here to question her freedom—
Without thinking about…
 How it will lead her to question herself yet again.

EMPATHS

Empaths are not told to understand everything,
Yet they do—because they are made like this.
They understand everything,
Yet they are deeply cut too.

Empaths are always paired with non-empaths,
Making it a living hell ride for them!
If it is important to me, then it is!
Why, when you say things that give us a wound,
Is nothing for you ?

While you don't see the things that keep us happy,
Feeling too much is a curse according to you.
What about when you don't consider anything we feel?
A massive destruction —
We feel everything, and you feel nothing.

What should be horrendous, you say?
We love, we value,
But you don't—
You just ramp over it, losing those who get you without
asking...
While we remain on the edge,
Begging to be understood the way we deserve,
Not the way you want.

CONTRASTS

Flowers, hair clips, and hairbands
Are the things that adorn her hairstyles...
She's soft because she chooses to be!
She saw she didn't get one, so she became one!

Not that she can't be fierce,
Or she is always timid.
She lifts weights, office files,
And cooks hot food for you...

That's not all .
She is much more than this!
But your lenses only see 1.5x zoomed.
To truly see her,
Sit next to her, listen to her,
Observe her, and see the magic, darling...

Some stay home, some go out,
But all are fighting alone inside—
Because they see what the outside holds for them.

Some get hands to hold,
Some get touched without consent.
Some breathe fresh air,
Some get choked behind closed doors.

Some get adorned with flowers at baby showers,
Some get killed without flowers on their bodies when
they die...

When will the contrast change, and by whom?
Someone who will forget superiority,
And embrace her with love —
Then, it will change, I feel!

WILDFLOWER'S TALE
Wildflowers bloom the prettiest
With the little that they get.

They also perish if ramped!
We admire them for growing again in the wild—
Bouncing back, resilient enough...

But the real question is,
Do we really need to be one?
Where we adjust with little and bloom for others,
Forgetting what we need to bloom...

Nature will also teach you
Not to follow their path sometimes.
What they couldn't do for themselves,
Do it for yourself.

Turn the tables, please—
It's high time now, honeypie...

WATER AT NIGHT
When I see water at night,
my body trembles…
Feels like someone exposed me—bare, open—
with my fears and insecurities coming to my calm shores in
waves.

My body aches with the pain buried—
the pain I tried facing.

Sometimes I face it proudly.
Sometimes I fail miserably.

Water at night is an overthinker's mind at night.
Looks still from the outside,
but if you tap it lightly—
the waves will gulp you along.

Because every night,
overthinkers are pulled in by their thoughts—
making them stiff and shocked.

If alive with everything at night,
you will see them early in the morning, in sunlight—
as if the darkest night went by.

But who will tell them?

That water at night is the same—
all the time.

P.O.V OF THE PEOPLE ON WHEELS
International Day of Persons with Disabilities it was this year
—

yet it is too difficult for us to choose ourselves often.

Because we constantly need help—
to even survive.

All praise for those who take care—
or should we say choose to take care?

Nobody talks about how we choose to survive.
That's why we are seen alive.

Often, love is degraded to just taking care.
When all we need is emotional and mental support—
along with basic needs to be met.

Never seen as grown-ups,
or even as individuals.
Because if you take care—
I must still be a baby!

If, in all of this, we dare choose ourselves,
we are terribly labeled—
as ungrateful.

If you see us this way,
don't pretend to be inclusive please!
Don't pretend to be empathetic enough to even consider us.

You don't allow us to breathe—
God does.

So stop hyping us simply, if you can't do what's necessary.

DREAMS TURNED INTO HORROR
She dreamt of saving lives.
But her own life was taken away.

We protest.
We voice out.
But nothing changes—why?
Ever thought of it?
Yes, we think… and then forget.

The root cause must be seen deeply,
Uprooted permanently.

How? Let me tell you today.

Sensitization is one step.
Awareness—real awareness—is the main character.
About everything.
About periods.
About what women deserve.
About what men deserve too.

Education starts at home,
And behaviors are modeled first by parents,
Then by friends.

Fixing a child's mindset before they grow up—
That alone can save so much.

Gender biases,
Planted at home,
Grow into deep-rooted mindsets.

See how a husband behaves in front of his children.
If he fails to set the right example,
Step away. Teach them separately.

So that growing boys don't grow up , to normalize what scars
someone else's daughter.

The root cause?
A society already conditioned.
Laws written but ignored.
Politics woven into injustice.
The silence of bystanders.

Waiting for someone to save you—
That, too, can be a cause.

That's why learning self-defense,
Speaking up without guilt,
Rejecting the narrative
That victims are to be blamed ,
Can save you.
Can save this country.
Policies won't fix everything. Uprooting the cause will.

THE DIFFERENCE CURSE BEGINS AT HOME
Gender biases start at home—
right from the day you choose Team Pink or Blue at your
baby shower.
I know it's just a ritual for some,
but that shows how deeply it's engraved in your brain.

To be gender-neutral—bring all kinds of toys...
be it cars, trucks, or dolls.

When parents-to-be have conversations,
let it be framed like this:
"Whoever it will be, it will be ours.
We will raise a human—beyond genders and their
norms!"

The entire family should be counseled
before they have a say in the new parents' matters...
that's how you will not pass the difference curse
to your next generations.

And trust me—
it will hit you differently.

SUICIDE PREVENTION – A NEED OF THE HOUR

Suicide becomes their last option,
not because they never tried,
but because no one truly listened—
yet advice comes for free.

Don't you think they fought every battle
before they finally freed themselves?
All they wanted was to be heard,
but instead, they were judged for free.

Have you ever spun on a giant wheel?
Felt the dizzying speed,
your head trapped in an endless spiral?
That's what their thoughts do to them.

They just want it to stop,
but seeking therapy is still a taboo.

Why would they want to survive,
when chaos exists in two places—
one in the world,
and the other in their mind?

What can be done to stop it?
Give them a space where they can speak freely.
Understand that their struggles
are not just "drama"—
They are battles unseen.

Awareness is the first step—
for them, around them,
before it's too late.

WE SHARE, WE GROW!
Sometimes, your inner battles
are the biggest monsters you'll have to fight.
Figuring it out alone?
 Kudos, bro.
But why struggle alone
when you have genuine people around?

Crying in silence works for a while,
but the only way out is to release the uneasiness stirring
inside you.

Genuine people aren't the ones
who provide you with everything—
they are the ones who don't put you down for sharing
what you feel.

Trust me, your feelings are valid
because you are valid and real.
There's no shame in feeling the way you do!

Today, promise yourself
that you will be happy—
because you want to survive,
because you deserve to survive!

Let's live beyond our survival mode.
That's why when we share, we grow!

76

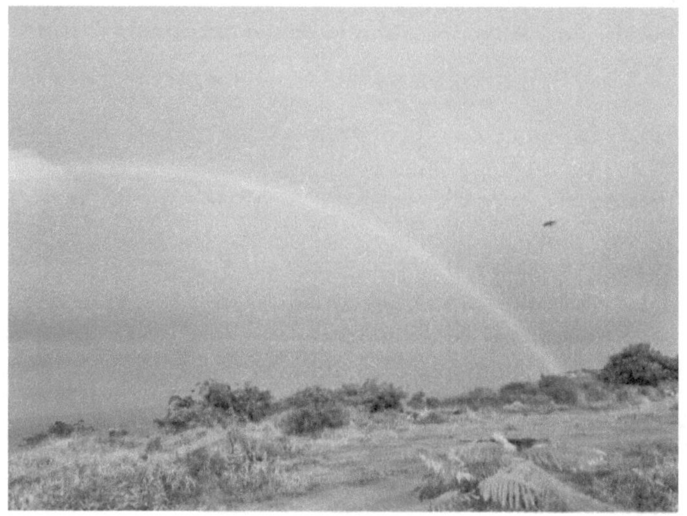

4. MUSINGS & WHISPERS

UNTAMED WHISPERS

Untamed whispers are like a gentle breeze that you feel
on your face,
a strand of your hair moved by the wind .
Like someone whispering sweet nothings in your ear,
making you giggle straight away!

Untamed whispers are raw, real truths spoken without
fear,
not letting others control what you should say!
You tell it fiercely, yet softly,
but you say it and just walk away.

It doesn't matter how it is received—
After all, it's the truth that whispers won't be able to hold
it for too long.

TENDER COCONUT TALES
A coconut is termed as harsh outside, soft inside,
but a tender coconut?
It defends itself by looking unripe, hard.

Yet when you open it—
it's bliss for those who love nature, water, and the tender
malai inside.

The soft malai proves—
however hard you might be,
your softness will always be valued by the right people.

The ones who will cherish every part of you,
like a tender coconut lover!

Whether you buy it at the beach or from the market,
Everyone relishes it, despite its 'sakht launda image' !

Grind it.
Make ice cream.
Drink it.

Either way,
you'll always be in the tender coconut's team.
Accept it—
or just relish it, babe!

CAN I CALL YOU ROSE?
Can I call you Rose?

Because—OH MY GOD—
What in the world is that red beauty? please —
blooming in my cozy place?

Every day, talking to you—
asking how you've been.
Do you need something?

Watering you with my own hands—
watching you glow,
proving that you don't just need basic things to survive.

You need conversations.
Care.
Love.

To feel truly seen—
to grow,
thrive,
and bloom in your own glory.

MIRRORS DON'T LIE
Mirrors are the same for everyone,
Be it greens or you!
Then why not see ourselves the way we do in the mirror?
Or are we too interested in how people perceive us,
Ready to lose ourselves
In the circle of judgment?

MOONOLOGY
The moon needs no introduction.
It gives the spotlight to others,
Knowing that people will love it from afar.

But it stays close to those who are moon lovers,
and have their lovers.

It's easy to admire the moon
When you don't see its blemishes.
But the moon doesn't mind—
It shines for all,
Even those who don't accept it as it is.

If the moon appears half or full,
We make days for it too.
Its light difference is also our issue.
When will we see things as they are?

PARADISE
One day at a time,
Hold yourself tight.
If there is rain,
Soon, you will see a rainbow.

That's your life—
A paradise in itself.
One day at a time,
That's how your life is a paradise.

CHEESECAKE
A bed of crumbled biscuits of your choice, set with
melted butter—
as if beginning the most epic saga of love that will melt
in your mouth.

Topped with cream cheese,
 homemade or store bought, mixed with fresh cream.
Ahh! Sounds like a twist of richness about to grace your
tongue soon!

Pour your favorite toppings, or infuse it with chocolate
ganache or coffee flavor—
the choice is yours!

The tough part of this epic taste blast is refrigerating it
for hours to set it.
before you gulp it down in no time!

No bake cheesecake? Or wait till it sets—what saga will
it be?

TIRAMISU DELIGHT
Tiramisu was always a pick me up dessert,
but the way it elevated my taste buds was insane.

Rich coffee blended with a soft sponge bed underneath,
fresh cream with favorite toppings—
heaven for a coffee lover and a delight for every sweet
tooth.

A one time experience for someone who just tried,
a lifetime favorite dessert for a coffee lover.

A NEW DAWN OF REALIZATION
After 25 years of celebrating your birthdays,
you realize that you want something different.
Your thought process changes,
the way you look at life changes!

You accept harsh truths,
you don't settle for things that are not your peace.
You refuse to tear apart in pieces.

A new dawn of realization hits.
You settle for love that brings peace.
You do things that make you happy.

CHOSEN BEFORE KNOWING

In a world full of ifs and buts,
Let's just soak in what we trust.

When peace settles within,
when the restless mind slows—
when something reaches your eyes,
and, for once,
the noise quiets...

Then keep it.
Fight for it.
Let the endless monologues
rest in peace.

Choose it—
because it chose you first,
long before you even knew.

THOUGHTS THAT KILL THE ACTION
Have you ever thought about something so much
that you drop the idea of doing it?
Because you think of its consequences
long before their time, baby!

But let me tell you one thing—
nobody will think about it as much as you do.
That only proves…
you keep your moral values intact,
or rather, conditioned for everything—badly!

But who's the moral police
in a society where everything you do
is always wrong in different ways,
through different eyes?

So, will you choose it,
or will you drop it?
If you're minding your business,
not harming anyone physically,
If it gives you some peace,
then just do it—
because all egos get touched
when you finally breathe freely!

THE TOUCH OF SENSES

Have you ever seen the touch-me-not plant?
The moment you touch them, they respond.
It depends on who touches them,
As if they can sense whether they feel safe or threatened
by it.

They are not timid—let me tell you that!
They are created like that.

In the same way, a soft-hearted person is bare and
open...
They sense every gaze they encounter,
Feel everything in depth.

They just need a different environment to grow and stay,
Otherwise, they will curl up and shrink.

ROSES: LOVE IN FAREWELL

Roses are red,
People buy them to show love, to confess love to their
significant others.
They're also put in the hair to enhance the beautiful you!
When you are about to start your life journey with
someone, you decorate the entire room.

Roses are used in as many traditional ways as possible!
Everywhere you see roses, because they are called the
flowers of kings and queens!
But have you ever seen someone shower their love for
the last time on their loved ones with roses?
What if we gave them roses when they are leaving us for
their final abode,
to remind them they were loved, like before, and will be
loved forever?

THE BEST VERSION OF YOU
People say true love doesn't change you.
True! But it gently pushes you to become a better
version of yourself.
They already see the best in you,
Making you question your old patterns that once held
you back.

You might look at yourself and think you're not enough,
But this love will teach you that you've always been
enough.
Now, live for yourself,
And embrace the future you're meant to create.

THE BEST KIND OF WRAPS
The best kind of wraps are made with the goodness of
your favorite veggies,
Meat, and anything you love, with pita bread as its base.
Cucumber, carrots, and everything locked in,
Stuffed with lettuce leaves and mayo for the taste.

Oh! The yummiest one to go in your tummy, I bet.
Stuffed, grilled, or baked to perfection,
Charred just enough to blow you off your chair.
Your taste buds will clap, and your senses will be
elevated...

You'll want to have it again and again.

EXERCISE : A FUN SESSION

Not everyone can do Pilates,
Neither dumbbells.
Exercise should not feel like just exercise,
It should be a fun session for your soul to revive!

Doing it at your own pace and space is important.
Sweating and feeling good after it should be your only
goal.
When this is achieved, you will see the progress
naturally.

Dancing is also a workout, I swear...
Join Zumba and shake your legs!
Staying active and fit is all you need.
If needed, choose running instead!

THE ART OF HUMILITY

When you sit to view the sun before it sets,
You can't see it for long because it shines too bright for your
eyes.

Likewise, people rising up won't suit everyone,
Pricking their eyes...

That doesn't mean the sun won't shine!
But the same sun knows to set, humbling himself.

This proves that if you keep doing what's necessary,
You will shine no matter what!

Just be your humble self always,
Even at your peak...

DRIFTING APART
There will be a time when you will outgrow some
people.
It will be your best friend that you thought...
Or other people in relation to you...

There will be no prior hints to these fallouts.
Even if you try catching it while you slip,
They will still go ahead, leaving you to wonder where
you lacked?

You may try to get back, but that's it — they won't come,
even if you beg.

For the longest time, I thought it's my fault.
But it was an inevitable event that now occurred!
It starts with a lack of effort , you putting a little extra of
it.
That's why it kept hanging till it dropped and you were
not even aware of it.

Leave them. Those who want to stay will show you that
they love to stay with you,
Because they can't imagine their life without you...

THE DESIRE FOR SIMPLICITY

When she didn't know,
She was scared to dream,
Because her dreams weren't conventional enough
To be considered big,
But were definitely trivialized.

She didn't want money to be chased—
She just needed to fulfill the small things,
The things that brought happiness to her plate,
With desserts and roses in her vase,
On a daily basis.

She dreamt of traveling to her favorite city,
With the support she needed,
Yet maintaining her autonomy.
She wanted a connection that felt like home—
That's all.

She was bound by the ropes of "should" and
"shouldn't,"
Trying to please others,
But her heart longed for freedom,
To follow the path that felt true to her soul.

Yet, she loved the moon and stars,
With poetry that gave her peace.
She was too unique to even breathe slowly—
At her own pace.

All she wanted was love and support,
Which she found later in her life.
And now, she holds it dearly,
No matter what .

IKIGAI – THE REASON TO BE
Ikigai refers to the reason for your being.
The reason that excites you to wake up in the morning.
Your purpose to look forward in life ahead.

It gives you purpose to live beyond your monotonous
life—
Greenery, traveling, or anything that makes you scream
in excitement.
Everything counts...

The skills that get you paid.
The person who makes you the happiest is the sixer hit
in the stadium!

So whatever, or whoever, is your Ikigai...
Hold them tight, even if the bridge starts shaking.
Because they are the reason your heart beats and
breathes.

GREEN FLAG HUMANS

Green flag humans
are raised by the dedicated owners
of green gardens...

Where they trim and groom
their beloved trees—
just enough,
so they don't cross their growing place
and trouble others.

They will give you shade,
offering you the importance that you deserve .

No matter what happens,
they will help you see yourself
in their shade—
in any season.

The green forest recognizes its favorites,
giving their all to love you
and letting you love yourself too.

They see beyond
what you might whisper
to that green tree of yours.

TUNES THAT LINGER

Have you ever stumbled upon a song by accident?
That really hits your dopamine—and then it's on loop for
so long,
Eventually everyone around you gets bored listening to
it, hahaha!
But not you.

Over time, you will get a new song
to listen to on loop...
But there are certain songs
that never go out of your mind—
Neither does it leave your playlist.

Those feel like home
when you need to return back.

ONE YEAR OF SOMETHING NEW

One year of doing something new,
 something that she never thought of.
 It shaped her into a better human,
 teaching her to handle pressure like never before!
 Her knowledge reservoir was enhanced .
 about the outcome she never bothered,
In the process of it, she was so involved— it was tied to
her biggest dream though.
With time, life took its course,
 only for her to realize
that it was just an experience that she deserved .

BEYOND THE SURFACE

Those random wild flower trees—in the middle of the
street.
You will not even know about them until you stop and
look at them.
Maybe, that is when you will notice how unique they
are.

It happens with humans too!
You need to just see them beyond what they show to
you.
For that, you need to uncover their experiences gently
with them...

See something that needs to be seen—and then push
them into the wild.
To let them be free.

DANDELION HEART

Dandelions - softer than the feathers.
Winds take them away, yet they add beauty to the wild!
That's what a kind-hearted person does to the crowd.
Smile warmer than the sun,
Those shiny eyes which hold a reservoir for kindness.
Even if you borrow it from them,
You will be filled with it—without emptying them.
Oh, to have them by your side...
You will fly like the dandelions in the wild.
Hold them gently, because they know to stay when they
are loved right.

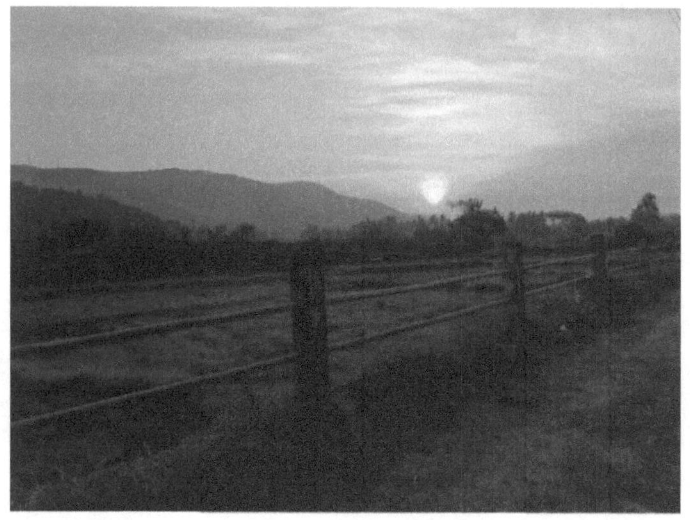

5. TERRA VERDE

SUN WORTH IT!
The sun wanted to kiss the water,
But was hesitant enough.
That's why it saw its own reflection in the water,
Realizing, I am worthy enough!

Even though some burn when I shine,
Some soak in my warmth,
Some catch the tan,
And some worship me effortlessly.

No matter what others perceive,
I will always remain the OG.
This shows—no matter what people say,
You will shine,
Because you are born to shine,
And be someone's sunshine.

VIEW THE MUSE
A landscape so green,
With the sun setting in,
Peeping through,
Wanting to know who's the best.

Oh! How to tell them both,
That when we draw landscapes like this,
We draw both.

A field, fenced across,
Yet, we see through it while we travel.
Wanting to touch, but keeping it sacred.
Touching through my eyes, etching it in my soul.
Writing through words,
Because I drank the view enough,
To write about it when it hits me harder.

HOMECOMING TO NATURE
Homecoming to nature is always more than an escape
from the noise around—
it's where my soul belongs.

The rustling of leaves is a drumroll to my entrance in
nature.
It's not a place I go when I'm bored;
It's the core of my very existence.

The way leaves, sky hues, flowers, and sunsets soothe
my soul—
as I soak them in with my eyes and capture them—
no one else is allowed to do the same.

Because I'm the VIP in their clan,
the Queen in her safe place.

No facades, no masks.
I'm allowed to be vulnerable because they know my
innocence is rare.

So nature steps in, to protect it—
becoming my muse to adore, write about, and love.

My screams are not reduced here; they are elevated
without shame.

My whole existence loves them—
from their roots to their gorgeous swatches of leaves.

WHEN GREENS AND SUNSET FLIRT
My heart bursts when I see greens,
and the sunset that flirts!
Behind the greens, when the sunset hides,
it leaves orange hues—
as if it reaches its peak orgasm,
making everything around beautiful.

The same way people take credit
for their help they did long ago,
only to bring it up later in ugly fights!

The sunset needs the greens to hide,
and the greens need the sunset for styling,
letting its hues color the leaves as they grow.

We all need each other—
or else, stay alone like apes back in the day .
It's a cycle, a circle—never half, but whole.
Two sides helping each other,
that's why the earth is round,
not a half-earth at all…

SERENE ESCAPE

I went to the greenest place ever—
where greens stretched longer than my eyelashes.

Down below, the greens met the beach,
open enough to get scared, maybe.

At the end of it, the gorgeous hues of the sun were seen!
It showed me what heaven usually looked like...

Wanted to stay there, placing a tent—
grass at the side, while you roll on the pebble path!

Each angle captured—never deleted, even if it was
needed.

THE GOLDEN RAYS...

The golden rays are proof of your amazing days coming
in.
Just be patient and enjoy the sun, and let it soak in.
If the sun sets, it's time to prepare for the next morning.
Every time we think it's over, it comes in with a new
day—a new bloom of the flowers that you see,
and your cheeks choose to blush all pink.
It's not over till you finish your breathing.

The future is what you look at when the sun rises,
and the past is all about that which you forget while
watching a sunrise and its hues in detail...

SUNLIGHT SERENE

You are something else, my heart said.
You are the sunlight beam that glows on me.
I met my best version when I met you, finally...
There is something unique I felt with you by my side.
I finally believed in magic
Because you are the one that I experienced.
You are amazing, oh my god!

A HOME OF PETALS

She loved flowers so much
that she would build her home
with all the flowers available in the market.

Wake up to the bunch of fresh white roses
in her favorite glass vase at her side table...

Buttercups for her green lawn garden for sure.

Plumeria—for the beachy feel days,
woven into her open wavy hair!

Roses tucked in her hair
when she is in a sleek red saree—
draped in love for a party to attend.

Rose petals scattered in her bathtub,
where she regains herself every day in the water.

Marigold—to let her go on the merry-go-round, she
promised.

Bougainvillea—for that aesthetic touch
and the softest feel from their petals.

Blue pea flower—for the natural stain of happiness,
and tea out of it in her cup!

That's how much she loves flowers...
All the flowers in her list—
till she exists and breathes , she promised .

UNTAMED WHISPERS

ABOUT THE AUTHOR

Vinita Bicholkar, who writes under the pen name VINI, is an Indian poetess, counselor, and an observer of life. Living life on wheels has never confined her; instead, it has shaped her perspective, allowing her to see beauty in the smallest moments.

Her poetry is a reflection of everything she observes, experiences, and imagines—crafted with raw emotions and a deep understanding of the world around her. As she grows, so will her poetry—flowing like an unending river, carrying the essence of her journey within every word.

Untamed Whispers is her debut poetry book, a collection of verses that speak from the soul, capturing the quiet, the raw, and the untamed souls.